CAREER PROFILES™

ANDERSON COOPER

Profile of a TV Journalist

Stephanie Watson

ROSEN
PUBLISHING®

New York

To my husband and son, for their enduring patience and support

Published in 2008 by The Rosen Publishing Group, Inc.
29 East 21st Street, New York, NY 10010

First Edition

Library of Congress Cataloging-in-Publication Data

Watson, Stephanie, 1969–
Anderson Cooper : profile of a TV journalist / Stephanie Watson.
— 1st ed.
        p. cm. — (Career profiles)
Includes bibliographical references and index.
ISBN-13: 978-1-4042-1907-6
ISBN-10: 1-4042-1907-2
1. Cooper, Anderson. 2. Television journalists—United States—
Biography. I. Title.
PN4874.C683W38 2008
070.92—dc22
[B]

                                                        2006039715

Manufactured in Ma aysia

CONTENTS

INTRODUCTION

The date was September 1, 2005.
Anderson Cooper, host of the Cable
News Network (CNN) newscast
Anderson Cooper 360°, was reporting
from Waveland, a historic seaside
town along the Mississippi Gulf Coast.
Just three days earlier, a storm surge
30 feet (98 meters) high from
Hurricane Katrina had nearly wiped
the town off the map.

   On August 29, Katrina had made
landfall near Buras, Louisiana. It was a
Category 3 hurricane with sustained
winds of 125 miles (201 kilometers)
per hour. The eye of the hurricane
passed just to the east of New Orleans,
lashing the city with battering winds

Anderson Cooper, who is seen here in June 2004 covering the funeral of President Ronald Reagan, has reported many breaking news stories for CNN.

and pounding rain. Water started spilling over the large dams, or levees, that had been designed to prevent the flooding of New Orleans, which is below sea level. Many levees broke, leaving 80 percent of the city underwater. After pummeling New Orleans, Hurricane Katrina blew into Mississippi. In the span of just a few hours, the hurricane killed more than 1,000 people and left at least 800,000 homeless along the Gulf Coast.

On September 1, three days after Hurricane Katrina made landfall, the region was still in chaos. In New Orleans, about 20,000 people remained in the Superdome sports stadium, where they had taken refuge shortly before the storm. The stadium was without electricity, adequate food and water, and medicine. Looting was rampant in the city, and police and rescue workers were being forced to dodge sniper fire. In Mississippi, much of the coastline lay in ruins and thousands of people were missing.

For the past fourteen years, Anderson Cooper had reported from some of the most dangerous and devastated spots in the world. He had covered famine in the African country of Niger. He had given reports on the wars in Iraq, Bosnia and Herzegovina, and Rwanda. He had covered the tsunami that had killed thousands of people in South Asia. Still, the destruction in the Gulf Coast after Hurricane Katrina was among the worst he had ever seen.

Cooper had spent three days traveling through Mississippi and capturing the storm's devastation on camera. He had seen the hope—and the desperation—of people who were searching for their belongings and for loved ones. They had shared with him their frustration that the U.S. government wasn't doing more to help in the recovery efforts.

On September 1, Cooper was in Waveland interviewing Senator Mary Landrieu of Louisiana, who had joined him remotely from Louisiana's capital city, Baton Rouge. He asked the senator whether the government bore responsibility for the lack of response to Katrina, and whether it should apologize for the chaos in New Orleans. Smoothly, Landrieu replied that there would be time to discuss the issues later. She began praising government officials and the Federal Emergency Management Agency (FEMA) for the great job they were doing in New Orleans. Then Cooper did something few reporters do—he cut in. In a voice shaking with undisguised anger, Cooper said, "Excuse me, Senator. I'm sorry for interrupting. I haven't heard that because, for the last four days, I've been seeing dead bodies in the streets here in Mississippi. And to listen to politicians thanking each other and complimenting each other, you know, I got to tell you, there are a lot of people here who are very upset and very angry and very frustrated . . . Do you get the anger that is out here?"

In the aftermath of Hurricane Katrina, Anderson Cooper was not just a journalist reporting on a story. He was a part of the story, and a voice for the millions of people who sat at home, watching the events unfold after the storm. For those observing him on television that day, it might not have been obvious that he was the child of American royalty, born into one of the wealthiest families in American history. The reason viewers may not have known Cooper's lineage was that he never used his famous family name as a springboard. He relied on his passion, his intellect, and his instincts to become one of the best-known anchors on television.

ONE

THE VANDERBILT LEGACY AND A PRIVILEGED CHILDHOOD

In 2004, when Anderson Cooper was a rising star at CNN, a portrait of the great shipping and railroad magnate Cornelius "Commodore" Vanderbilt (1794–1877) hung in the foyer of his New York studio apartment. Cornelius Vanderbilt—patriarch of one of the wealthiest and most powerful families in the United States—was Anderson's great-great-great-grandfather.

The Vanderbilt family is among the most prominent industrialist lineages, an American dynasty that amassed vast fortunes and achieved significant political and social influence. Many consider these families, which also include the Rockefellers (Standard Oil

Company), the Carnegies (U.S. Steel), and the Gettys (Getty Oil Company), as the American equivalent to royalty. These families have much in common: wealth, power, and philanthropy. They also share an entrepreneurial spirit; the founders of these industrial dynasties worked extremely hard and took huge risks to earn their fortunes.

Cornelius "Commodore" Vanderbilt

Cornelius "Commodore" Vanderbilt possessed this pioneer spirit. Cornelius was a descendant of Jan Aertsen Van der Bilt. Van der Bilt was a Dutchman who, in the middle of the seventeenth century, immigrated to New Amsterdam (the town founded on Manhattan Island and later renamed New York) in search of opportunity. The family eventually changed its name to Vanderbilt and settled in the waterfront town of Port Richmond, Staten Island, which is where Cornelius was born in 1794. He was the fourth of nine children. His father, Cornelius, was a farmer and ferryman. His mother, Phebe, ran the household.

Cornelius "Commodore" Vanderbilt (1794–1877), the shipping and railroad magnate, was Anderson Cooper's great-great-great grandfather.

At age eleven, Cornelius quit school to help out in his father's ferry business. Although he wasn't a good student, young Cornelius knew just about everything there was to know about boats, currents, channels, and tides. In 1810, when he turned sixteen, he borrowed money from his mother to buy a two-masted boat called a periauger, which he named the *Swiftsure*. He used it to ferry people and goods from Staten Island and Brooklyn to Manhattan. Cornelius surpassed his competitors by offering luxury service for a fraction of their price. During the War of 1812, when the British fleet blocked New York Harbor, Cornelius used his boat to transport workmen and supplies to U.S. military garrisons around the harbor. His willingness to sail in dangerous waters earned him a fortune, as well as the nickname "Commodore." In the late 1820s, Cornelius started his own steamboat business. By the 1840s, he had a fleet of more than 100 steamboats, and he was worth more than $1 million.

In the 1850s, Cornelius expanded into a new business: railroads. Within two years, he had consolidated the New York and Harlem, Hudson River, and New York Central Railroads into one train system that stretched across the Northeast, carrying passengers and freight. To house his train service, Cornelius

Cornelius Vanderbilt's mansion, photographed here circa 1920, took up an entire block along Fifth Avenue in New York City

built the massive brick-and-granite station, Grand Central Depot, on Forty-second Street and Fourth Avenue in Manhattan, at a cost of $6.4 million. It was the largest train terminal in the world at the time. (In 1903, it was rebuilt as Grand Central Station, which remains standing today.) When he died in 1877, Cornelius Vanderbilt had an empire that was worth nearly $100 million. He was the richest person in the United States.

Meet the Vanderbilts

William Henry Vanderbilt (1821–1885) was one of Cornelius Vanderbilt's thirteen children and his first son. William increased the number of railroads in his father's company, doubling his father's wealth. In 1880, he brought the ancient Egyptian obelisk known as Cleopatra's Needle from Egypt to Central Park in New York City.

Cornelius Vanderbilt II (1843–1899) was the oldest of William Henry Vanderbilt's eight children. In 1885, he bought and expanded the Breakers, a mansion overlooking the Atlantic Ocean in Newport, Rhode Island. It was one of the grandest homes in Newport and became one of the most visited homes by tourists in the United States.

George Washington Vanderbilt II (1862–1914) was the youngest son of William Henry Vanderbilt. From 1889 to 1895, George undertook the building of the Biltmore Estate in Asheville, North Carolina. Modeled after the great French châteaux of the Loire Valley, the Biltmore was the largest house that had ever been built in the United States, and it was the most lavish of all the Vanderbilt mansions.

Gertrude Vanderbilt Whitney (1875–1942) was the daughter of Cornelius Vanderbilt II. She was a sculptor, a major patron of the arts, and the founder of the Whitney Museum of American Art in New York City, which opened in 1931.

Poor Little Rich Girl

Gloria Vanderbilt was born on February 20, 1924, in Newport, Rhode Island, to Gloria Morgan, an eighteen-year-old socialite, and Reginald Claypoole Vanderbilt, the youngest son of Cornelius Vanderbilt II and Alice Claypoole Gwynne. Almost immediately after Gloria's birth, her mother and father departed for Europe to help her mother recuperate from the difficult delivery. The Vanderbilts left baby Gloria in the care of her maternal grandmother, Laura Morgan,

Gloria Vanderbilt is photographed as an infant in 1925 with her parents, Gloria and Reginald Vanderbilt.

and her Irish nurse, Emma Sullivan Keislich, whom Gloria would later call Dodo. The Vanderbilts did not return from Europe until August. Little Gloria's grandmother and nurse became the only real parents she would know.

When Gloria was only fifteen months old, her father died from liver disease brought on by his frequent alcohol binges. For the next few years, Gloria accompanied her mother as she hopped from party to party in city after city. They journeyed to Monte Carlo, London, Paris, and Hollywood. Gloria's grandmother and Dodo traveled everywhere with them. According to *Fortune's Children* (1989), a book written by Arthur T. Vanderbilt, Grandmother Morgan was not pleased with her daughter's decadent lifestyle.

Grandmother Morgan was so upset by her daughter's apparent lack of interest in little Gloria that she devised a plan for her beloved granddaughter's care. She enlisted the help of Gloria's aunt, a tall and imposing woman named Gertrude Vanderbilt Whitney. What ensued was

Gloria Vanderbilt *(left)* poses in the early 1940s with her aunt, Gertrude Vanderbilt Whitney. Whitney had won a bitter legal battle to gain custody of her niece in 1934.

a bitter custody battle over ten-year-old Gloria. It began on October 1, 1934, during the height of the Great Depression, when many people in the United States were left unemployed and homeless in the wake of the 1929 Wall Street stock market crash. Americans wanted something to think about other than their poverty and misery. The story was splashed on the front pages of tabloid newspapers, and the public was spellbound by the sensational and scandalous trial. Onlookers and reporters mobbed the courtroom. The newspapers began referring to Gloria as the "Poor Little Rich Girl."

On November 21, 1934, the judge announced his decision—he gave Gertrude Vanderbilt Whitney custody of the child. Gloria went to live at her aunt Gertrude's estate in Old Westbury, New York. As her aunt's ward, Gloria had a very strict upbringing. Although she had the run of the enormous estate and was constantly attended to by a fleet of maids, chauffeurs, and bodyguards, Gloria received very little affection from her aunt.

Hollywood Husbands

In June 1941, when Gloria turned seventeen, she went to stay with her mother in Beverly Hills,

California. It was a relief to escape from the confines of her aunt Gertrude's house, and, for the first time, to travel without a constant chaperone. Gloria had become a stunning woman; she had dark hair, porcelain skin, and almond-shaped eyes that gave her an exotic appearance. Gloria took full advantage of her beauty and wealth. She dated a string of celebrities, including actors Errol Flynn and Marlon Brando, singer Frank Sinatra, author Roald Dahl, and billionaire movie producer Howard Hughes.

In December 1941, Gloria settled down with a Hollywood talent scout, Pasquale "Pat" Di Cicco. Her wedding to Di Cicco was the first in a string of Hollywood marriages. She and Di Cicco divorced, and in 1945, she wed the world-famous conductor of the Philadelphia Orchestra, Leopold Stokowski. They had two children together—Leopold Stanislaus, born in 1950; and Christopher, born in 1955— before she and Stokowski divorced. In 1956, she married movie director Sidney Lumet, but they divorced in 1963. By the age of thirty-nine, Gloria Vanderbilt had been married and divorced three times. She just couldn't find the stable and loving home that she had yearned for all her life. Then she met Wyatt Emory Cooper.

Rich Little Poor Boy

Wyatt Cooper's life couldn't have begun more differently from Gloria Vanderbilt's. He was born in Quitman, Mississippi, in 1927, one of nine children of a poor farmer and his wife. What the family lacked in wealth, though, it made up for in history. Wyatt's paternal grandmother's family was among the first to settle in the Virginia Colony. His granduncle Jim Bull had fought with the Confederate army (the army formed by the Southern states that had seceded from the United States) in the 1863 Battle of Chickamauga during the Civil War (1861–1865).

As a child, Wyatt was a natural storyteller and actor. He gave guest sermons at Quitman's First Baptist Church when the preacher was away. Wyatt often hitched a ride into town to see *Gone with the Wind* and other films in Quitman's only movie theater. Although Wyatt's father wanted him to pursue a career in politics, Wyatt dreamed of becoming an actor.

In 1943, When Wyatt was sixteen, the Cooper family moved briefly to New Orleans. They lived in a ground-floor apartment in the Ninth Ward, and Wyatt attended Francis T. Nicholls High School. Wyatt loved New Orleans—he saw his first opera and his first ballet there, and he thought it was so much more exciting and exotic than Quitman. But the family eventually moved back to Mississippi, settling in the town of Meridian.

Wyatt ultimately left the South for the bright lights of Hollywood to pursue his dream. He acted in a few TV shows and commercials, but he couldn't really make it as an actor. He turned to screenwriting instead, working for the big Hollywood film studio Twentieth Century-Fox Film Corporation.

A Privileged Childhood

Gloria Vanderbilt and Wyatt Cooper met at a dinner party given by a mutual friend in New York. They were almost complete opposites: he had never been married and she had been married three times. He was from a poor family and she was from one of the wealthiest in the country. Still, they saw something special in each other. "There was something about his eyes," Vanderbilt told her son, Anderson, who recounted the story in his autobiography, *Dispatches from the Edge: A Memoir of War, Disasters, and Survival* (2006). "We were from two different worlds, but he understood me better than anyone else ever had." Gloria and Wyatt were married just before Christmas 1964.

On January 27, 1965, Gloria gave birth to a son, Carter Vanderbilt Cooper. Two years later, on June 3, 1967, she and Wyatt had another son, Anderson Hays Cooper. Anderson's first name was taken from the maiden name of Wyatt's mother. His middle name, Hays, came from Gloria's maternal grandfather, Harry Hays Morgan. From the start, the brothers were close. While his mother was pregnant, Carter nicknamed his brother "Baby Napoleon." When the boys got a bit older, Carter would stage big military campaigns, directing miniature armies of toy soldiers across their bedroom floor.

From a young age, Anderson and his brother understood that their family was wealthy. They lived in an elegant five-story mansion on the Upper East Side of Manhattan. Giant stone lions stood guard on either side of the entryway, and a huge marble staircase led upstairs. But Anderson realized even then that wealth did not bring happiness. He told Brad Goldfarb of *Interview* magazine in 2004 that his father's poor background felt more real to him than his mother's wealthy upbringing. "Certainly, growing

In 1972, Wyatt Cooper and Gloria Vanderbilt arrive at the premiere of a movie in New York City. They were married in 1964 and later had two sons, Carter and Anderson.

up, there was a nice apartment and nice things in the apartment. But for me, one of the greatest privileges of my background was realizing that what a lot of people think they want will not ultimately make them happier."

Anderson also realized early on that his mother was far from the typical soccer mom. "On report day at school, she'd show up dressed in a purple beaver-skin coat and matching stockings," he wrote in the April 2005 issue of *Details* magazine. "She's very cool, and way ahead of her time." Their relationship was often more like confidantes than mother and son. "I can talk to Anderson about anything," Vanderbilt told Jonathan Van Meter of *New York* magazine in September 2005.

Gloria Vanderbilt's friends were also far from typical. Author Truman Capote, artist Andy Warhol, and silent film actor Charlie Chaplin were frequent guests at the family's home. Anderson and his brother loved spending time with these famous people when they came to visit, although Warhol's brilliantly white hair scared Anderson, and Capote's lisp made him laugh, he recalled in *Dispatches from the Edge*. Gloria often thought Anderson might himself become an entertainer. She told *People* magazine in January 2001 that she had caught him once at around age eleven doing a "brilliant imitation of Dr. Ruth [Westheimer, the diminutive sex therapist and radio show host]."

Unlike many parents of that era, who sent their children off with babysitters when they had friends over, the Coopers welcomed their children to their parties. Anderson and Carter sat with the adults and were always invited to join in the conversation. According to the Van Meter article, Wyatt once said, "No child should ever be called little." In all Anderson and Carter did, their parents encouraged them to think independently. They also encouraged the boys to follow their dreams, whatever they may have been.

Dreams of the Future

Anderson's dream was to travel around the world. When he was just five or six years old, the acclaimed author Isak Dinesen gave his mother a globe. His mother gave that globe to Anderson, who placed the globe on a table next to his bed. At night, when he couldn't sleep, he could run his finger over the many countries that he longed to visit.

Anderson's other great love was television. He scheduled his entire afternoons around watching TV. From the time he got home from school until

Anderson and Carter are photographed during a playful moment with their parents in their Southhampton home on Long Island in 1972.

bedtime, all he wanted to do was watch his favorite programs. Anderson loved the *Andy Griffith Show*, the afternoon movie, a cartoon show called *Magilla Gorilla*, and especially the news programs. Anderson joked to a reporter at Mediabistro.com in 2004 that he'd been a news junkie since *before* he was born.

As a child, Anderson had a mild form of dyslexia, a reading problem that causes people to see letters and words in reverse. Consequently, he wasn't much of a reader or writer. He was in awe of his father's writing ability, though. While Wyatt was working on his book, *Families: A Memoir and a Celebration*, Anderson recalls coming into his father's study late at night when he couldn't sleep. "Laying my head against his chest, I could always fall asleep listening to the sound of the typewriter and the steady beat of his heart," he wrote in his May 2006 CNN.com blog. Anderson felt that to write a book would be the ultimate achievement. Although he couldn't write well when he was young, Anderson had the same creative spirit as his father. Eventually, his writing talent emerged and he, too, became a published author. Writing is just one of many traits father and son had in common. People have told Anderson that he has his father's sense of humor and passion for storytelling, according to a 2005 story in *New York* magazine. Physically, Anderson and his father also look strikingly similar. Anderson has the same intense blue eyes and the same determined stare, and he even parts his hair like his father did.

Wyatt Cooper left Anderson and his brother, Carter, with a strong sense of their family history.

When his book came out in 1975, Wyatt took the boys with him on speaking tours in Mississippi. They visited Wyatt's hometown of Quitman. Although the wooden house in which Wyatt was born was long gone by then, people in the small town remembered him, and they still called him by his childhood nickname, Buddy. When Anderson was nine years old, his father took him to New Orleans. They toured the historic French Quarter, which Anderson loved, and they posed together for a picture in a touristy old-time photo shop. In the antiqued sepia-toned picture, Wyatt wore a Confederate soldier's uniform and Anderson held an old shotgun.

It wasn't long before tragedy entered Anderson's home, however. In 1975, his father had a heart attack. Wyatt had a family history of heart problems—both his father and one of his sisters had died young of heart attacks. Although Wyatt survived his heart attack, he had another massive one just two years later. With each subsequent heart attack, he went in and out of intensive care. On the afternoon of

Gloria Vanderbilt Cooper shared a close bond with Anderson and Carter and encouraged them to follow their dreams.

January 5, 1978, doctors at New York Hospital rushed him into the operating room for heart surgery. He died on the operating table that night. Wyatt Cooper was just fifty years old.

Ten-year-old Anderson was asleep when his mother came into his room and told him that his father had died. "When my dad died, I felt like my life restarted," Anderson told *Time* magazine in June 2006. "The person I was disappeared, and this sort of new person was formed." Anderson and Carter never discussed their father's death—it was too painful. After the funeral, they were never again able to connect

When Anderson was nine years old, he and his father took a memorable trip to the French Quarter of New Orleans.

with each another emotionally the way they had done when they were younger.

Wyatt Cooper died young, but he didn't leave without saying good-bye. His farewell to his family was the book he wrote before his death, *Families: A Memoir and a Celebration* (1975). Anderson told *New York* magazine in 2005 that he still reads his father's book about once a year. For him, it's a way to remember the man he lost when he was just a boy. The book is filled with the guidance that Anderson believes his father would have given him through the years if he had lived longer.

The last sentence of the book was so meaningful to family members that they used it as the epitaph on Wyatt's tombstone: "We must go rejoicing in the blessings of this world, chief of which is the mystery, the magic, the majesty, and the miracle that is life."

TWO ANOTHER DEATH IN THE FAMILY

After his father's death, Anderson decided that he needed independence from his family. Although they had plenty of money, he was determined to earn his own living. The only trouble was, there weren't many jobs open to eleven-year-olds. (The legal working age in the United States is sixteen.) Consequently, Anderson applied for the only job he could get at the time, working as a model with the Ford Modeling Agency in New York. By the time he was twelve, he was modeling clothes for such well-known designers as Calvin Klein and Ralph Lauren. He also modeled for Macy's department

Anderson shakes hands with fashion designer Ralph Lauren during a runway show in 2006. When Anderson was twelve years old, he modeled for the eminent designer.

store. But at thirteen, he decided to leave the modeling industry. Determined to keep working while attending school, Anderson took jobs as a waiter and an office assistant.

School Days

Anderson attended the Dalton School, a private college-preparatory school (grades kindergarten through twelve) on the Upper East Side of Manhattan. The school, which emphasizes rigorous academics and the arts, has many celebrity alumni, including actors Chevy Chase and Mary Stuart Masterson and photographer Diane Arbus.

Anderson's high school experience went far beyond classes in math, science, and literature. He also took survival courses, went on month-long mountaineering expeditions in the Rocky Mountains, and participated in a sea-kayaking trip off the coast of Mexico. At age seventeen, he left high school a month early to go on a survival trip to Africa. He spent several months traveling by truck through the southern and central regions of the continent. In his book, *Dispatches from the Edge*, Anderson called Africa "a place to forget" and escape the pain of his father's death. Unfortunately, it was also a place where he became very ill. He was infected with malaria and had to spend time in a Kenyan hospital recuperating. Anderson didn't tell his mother about his illness until after he had returned home, covered in mosquito bites.

Anderson graduated from Dalton in 1984. The following year, he entered Yale University. There he studied political science and international relations. Anderson thought about becoming a diplomat and joining the U.S. Foreign Service, the part of the U.S. Department of State that sends American diplomats where they are needed abroad. Before he could

Going Gray

Gray hair is a physical feature that most people associate with growing old. But in certain cases, young people grow gray hair because cells in their hair roots stop producing the pigment melatonin. The cause is usually genetic, meaning it is inherited from one or both parents. Many people say prematurely gray hair makes a person look distinguished, sophisticated, or mature.

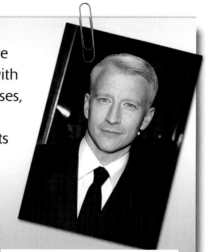

Cooper considers his prematurely gray hair both a blessing and a curse.

Anderson started going gray when he was just sixteen years old. He has never liked admitting that he has gray hair and prefers to refer to his signature hair color as salt-and-pepper. As he wrote in the August 2003 issue of *Details* magazine, "Gray is nature's way of whispering, 'You're dying.'" Nevertheless, Anderson admits, "in the TV news business, gray equals gravitas."

decide on a career, however, tragedy struck his family again.

Losing a Brother

During the summer of 1988, as part of his college political science major, Anderson served as an intern at the Central Intelligence Agency (CIA) headquarters in Langley, Virginia (a suburb of Washington, D.C.). Meanwhile his brother, Carter, who had graduated from Princeton University the previous year, was working as an editor for *American Heritage*, a history magazine based in New York. It was a difficult time for Carter—he had recently broken up with his girlfriend, and he was being treated by a therapist for depression.

On the morning of July 22, Carter showed up at his mother's penthouse apartment in Gracie Square, on Manhattan's Upper East Side, and announced that he was moving back in with her. His mother told him they could discuss the move over his favorite lunch, spaghetti with homemade sauce. While Gloria prepared lunch, Carter took a nap on Anderson's bed. Although the day was torturously hot, Carter refused to let his mother turn on the air-conditioning.

Around 7 PM, Carter came into his mother's room. As Gloria Vanderbilt recalled in *A Mother's Story* (1996), Carter looked disoriented and kept repeating, "What's going on? What's going on?" He appeared as though he had been taking drugs, but his mother did not believe that was the case because, she wrote, he barely drank alcohol and had no history of drug use. She tried to calm him, but he pulled away and ran up the stairs into Anderson's room. She found Carter on the balcony outside Anderson's room, sitting precariously on the stone wall that surrounded the terrace. She asked him what he was doing and tried to approach him, but he kept her at bay. Carter asked, "Will I ever feel again?" Suddenly, a plane flew overhead. Carter looked up at the flash of silver and then, as if it had been a sign, threw his body over the wall, hanging from its edge like a gymnast, according to Vanderbilt's account. He held on for a moment and then let go, falling fourteen stories to his death. Carter was just twenty-three years old. (In *A Mother's Story*, Vanderbilt wrote that she believed Carter's distorted mental state and suicide might have been triggered by a prescription medication he was taking for his asthma.)

Often, when the sibling of someone who has died is interviewed in the newspaper or on television, he or she will claim to have had a "feeling" at the precise moment when his or her sibling died. Anderson had no such preternatural inkling, he wrote in his *Details* magazine column in September 2003. By the time his mother was able to track him down in Washington, D.C., to tell him the tragic news, it had been several hours since his brother's death. Because it was too late for him to catch a flight back to New York, Anderson made the 250-mile (402 km) trip home by car.

In life, Carter had been a thinker and a dreamer. He had been a brilliant conversationalist, able to discuss history, literature, and many other topics with ease. But for Anderson, the shadow of his brother's suicide forever clouded his memory of Carter. "That's the thing about suicide. No matter how much you try to remember how that person lived his life, you can't forget how he ended it," Anderson wrote in *Dispatches from the Edge.*

Funeral services for Carter Cooper were held at the St. James Church on Madison Avenue. As Anderson helped his mother out of the car, photographers surrounded them. The paparazzi were like "vultures circling over weakened prey," Anderson wrote in a 2005 article in *Details* magazine. Many political and artistic luminaries attended the funeral, including First Lady Nancy Reagan, designer Bill Blass, publisher Malcolm Forbes, and *Cosmopolitan* magazine editor Helen Gurley Brown. At the funeral, Anderson read passages from works by F. Scott Fitzgerald, one of his brother's favorite authors. His voice cracking with emotion, he praised his brother's soul as being "golden and true," according to a 1988 article in the *New York Times.* "It's hard to

Cooper and his mother console each other after Carter's funeral in July 1988.

believe he's not going to wander in here absentmind-
edly, laugh good-naturedly, and apologize for all the
trouble he's caused, and then ask Mom to make him
some spaghetti," Anderson said. Carter was buried
alongside his father at the Moravian Cemetery in New
Dorp on Staten Island.

Coping with Tragedy

In the fall of 1988, it was time for Anderson to
return to Yale and begin his senior year. He wanted
to stay in New York and continue to comfort his

Cooper attended Yale University in New Haven, Connecticut, from 1984 to 1989, and graduated with a degree in political science.

mother, but she insisted that he return to college. Anderson's final year at Yale was a difficult one. He was still recovering from the loss of his brother and the residual pain he felt from his father's death. He became obsessed with wondering what drove his brother to take his own life. But in the spring of 1989, he did graduate from Yale, earning a bachelor of arts degree in political science. At Anderson's graduation, his mother gave him a piece of advice: "Follow your bliss," she said, quoting Joseph Campbell, an American professor and writer known for his works in mythology and comparative religion. Campbell once said, "When you follow your bliss . . . doors will open where you would not have thought there would be doors, and where there wouldn't be a door for anyone else."

The trouble was, Anderson hadn't yet found his bliss. His brother's death had distracted him from following his original political science career, and now he wasn't sure which profession he wanted to pursue. After graduation, Anderson took a year off while he decided what he would do with his life. Then a new career path began to take shape. While Anderson was in college, he had read quite a bit about the Vietnam War and the reporters who covered it. Reporting sounded to him like an adventure. The pain of war, he thought, might help him deal with the pain he felt inside. Anderson decided that he wanted to work in television news.

THREE

BREAKING INTO THE BUSINESS

Getting into the television news business proved more difficult than Cooper had anticipated. Typically, students leaving college with a degree in broadcast journalism either apply for an entry-level job as an assistant at a television station or start out in a small market. (Markets are ranked in the United States by the number of television-viewing households they contain, with New York and Los Angeles being the biggest markets in the country, and cities such as Mankato, Minnesota, and Fairbanks, Alaska, being among the smallest markets.)

Cooper had in his favor his family's friends in the entertainment industry, but his desire to be independent made him refuse to use any connections. "It just wasn't something I would've been comfortable with," he told Lianne George of *Maclean's* magazine in June 2006. Instead, he applied on his own to the ABC network for an entry-level position as news assistant. As is the case with many entry-level jobs in television, the main responsibilities included answering telephones and photocopying. But assistant jobs in television are highly competitive. Even with his Yale degree, Cooper didn't get the position.

A Risky Career Move

After a few months, he finally landed a job as a fact-checker for *Channel One News*, a twelve-minute newscast that airs in high school classrooms around the country. Cooper worked there for six months and then decided that what he really wanted to do was to travel abroad and report on wars. He quit his job, borrowed a friend's Hi-8 camera, and had that friend forge a fake press pass for him so that he could gain access to areas that were off-limits to the public. He hadn't studied how to shoot and edit stories in school or during an internship program at a television station, as many students do. Everything Cooper knew about

Channel One News and the network's Web site provide fast-breaking news and information about teen-related issues to young students.

reporting, he had learned solely from watching television news.

In December 1991, he flew to Thailand on his way to Burma (now known as the Union of Myanmar), the largest country in mainland Southeast Asia. A

1988 coup d'état in that country had put a brutal military regime in power. In Thailand, Cooper met up with Burmese students who were trying to overthrow the military dictatorship. The students helped sneak Cooper across the Thailand-Burma border so that he could shoot a story about their efforts. After editing his story, Cooper sent it to *Channel One News*. They bought it. He called his mother and said, "I think I've found my bliss," Cooper recalled in *Dispatches from the Edge*.

After leaving Burma, he traveled to Vietnam. He studied Vietnamese at the University of Hanoi while he shot and edited more stories for *Channel One News*. Cooper worked as a freelancer—*Channel One News* compensated him by the story, rather than paying him an annual salary. His handheld video technique, youth, and first-person reporting style were popular with both *Channel One*'s management and its viewers. "What he did here was not conventional," Jim Morris, co-executive producer at *Channel One News*, told *Electronic Media* magazine in 1997, "Our audience loved it."

A Country in Chaos

Cooper's next destination, in September 1992, was the East African nation of Somalia. For two years, the

Civilians in Rangoon, Burma, protest in 1988. The Burmese military put down civil unrest and soon took over the country.

country had been in turmoil, its population decimated by civil war and famine. Thousands of people had already died of starvation, and millions more were at risk. Cooper used his fake press pass to hitch a ride with a relief flight headed into Somalia. The plane was traveling to Baidoa, a city in south-central Somalia and one of the hardest-hit regions of the country. In August 1992, the population of Baidoa had been 37,000. Within three months, it had plummeted to 21,000, according to a December 1992 report by the U.S. Centers for Disease Control and Prevention.

In 1992, Cooper found a desperate situation in Baidoa, Somalia, where millions of people were at risk for starvation.

The relief plane dropped Cooper off, and he was left alone with a couple of thousand dollars in cash, a camera, and a backpack filled with cashews (the only food he'd had time to buy at the airport before boarding his original flight). He slept on the roof of a building and hitched rides wherever he needed to go. During the forty-eight hours he spent in Somalia, Cooper shot two emotional stories capturing the plight of the Somali people. One story showed a family burying the last of their four sons—a boy who was just five years old when he died.

Cooper's reports finally landed him a full-time job as a correspondent with *Channel One News* in late 1992. He was twenty-five years old. Despite the steady salary, Cooper didn't change his reporting style, still preferring to travel alone and shoot with the same home video camera. For the next two

In 1993, Cooper traveled to Sarajevo in Bosnia and Herzegovina, where he reported on the fighting between Bosnian Serbs, Bosnian Croats, and Muslims.

years, he traveled all over the world for *Channel One News* as its chief international correspondent. He went to Russia, Haiti, Israel, Ukraine, Cambodia, Indonesia, and South Africa.

Sniper Fire

Cooper put himself into many chaotic and dangerous situations for his reports. In March 1993, his destination was Bosnia and Herzegovina. Following the end of the Cold War and the collapse of the Communist system, the former country of Yugoslavia was divided. The republics of Bosnia and Herzegovina, Croatia, Macedonia, and Slovenia had declared their independence from Yugoslavia, which led to fighting among Bosnian Serbs, Bosnian Croats, and Muslims. During the war, there was rampant ethnic cleansing—the killing of one ethnic group to increase the population of another ethnic group—primarily committed by the Serbs. It was into this hostile region that Cooper traveled, landing in Sarajevo, the capital of Bosnia and Herzegovina. Even though he'd covered many perilous situations by this point, he was still afraid. "Anyone who tells you they aren't scared in a war zone is a fool or a liar, and probably both. The more places you've been, the more you know just how easy it is to get killed," he wrote in *Dispatches from the Edge.*

Cooper ate, worked, and slept in a protective Kevlar flak jacket. His base was the war-torn Holiday Inn, its shattered windows an obvious reminder that the hotel was a frequent target of sniper fire. One day, while recording a stand-up report on a street corner near the hotel, he heard a loud bang. A column close to where he was standing had been hit by a bullet. He ran behind a building for protection and recorded with his camera as snipers peppered the area with automatic gunfire.

On later trips, Cooper covered the genocide in Rwanda, when militias made up of members of the Hutu ethnic group massacred hundreds of thousands of minority Tutsis. He reported the violence that broke out during the 1994 elections in Soweto, South Africa—the first general elections to be held after the end of the racist apartheid system in that country. Cooper didn't decide to report from turbulent locations because he's a danger junkie. Instead, he is fascinated with the idea of survival. He also considers it a personal mission to tell the stories of people who are coping with tragic situations. "To me, there is value in bearing witness to what is happening to people who are living their lives with great dignity in the face of horror," he told Brad Goldfarb of *Interview* magazine in 2004.

Blue-Jeaned Correspondent

When he was out in the field shooting a story and during the short periods when he was at home in New York, Cooper's lifestyle was far from the privileged upbringing he'd had as Gloria Vanderbilt's son. He worked long hours, not stopping even on the weekends. To say that his living conditions were sparse would be an understatement. "All his apartment had in it was a mattress, a spoon, and a bowl," Jim Morris of *Channel One News* told *Electronic Media* in 1997. But Cooper loved his work.

A few months after Cooper's contract with *Channel One News* expired, a representative from ABC News called and asked to see his tape. Television reporters keep a tape, or demo reel, of reports they have

Cooper, who often wears blue jeans while reporting, prepares to leave Beirut, Lebanon, in July 2006, during battles between Israel and Hezbollah fighters.

done. A tape is the visual equivalent of a résumé, and it showcases the reporter's abilities on camera. Cooper sent the tape, and in 1995, just three years after ABC had rejected him for a news assistant job, the company hired him as a correspondent. At twenty-eight, he was one of the youngest correspondents ever to work for the network. The job was solely based in New York, which Cooper found a welcome respite from his constant travel of the previous three years. He was reporting for *World News Saturday/Sunday*, as well as for *World News Tonight*

Cooper and Alison Stewart coanchored ABC's offbeat, late-night news show *World News Now.*

with Peter Jennings. He also began filling in as coanchor of ABC's *World News Now*, a late-night, slightly offbeat news show covering everything from serious issues to pop culture.

As in the past, Cooper's reports were personal narratives shot on camcorders. He rejected the jacket-and-tie ensemble that most reporters wear in favor of flannel shirts, blue jeans, and boots. "I want my subjects to feel comfortable with me, and I think it would be artificial for me if I'm riding around with cops one night and show up in a shirt and tie," he told Jon Lafayette of *Electronic Media* in 1997. Cooper also projected a more relaxed persona in the anchor's chair. "I think the notion of a traditional anchor is fading away, the all-knowing, all-seeing person who speaks from on high," he told Mediabistro.com in 2004. "I think you have to be yourself, and you have to be real." Cooper's raw, honest delivery earned him both praise and criticism. Although the public embraced his approach, some members of the news media felt that his style was more MTV than substantive journalism.

Cooper and *The Mole*

By 2000, Cooper was anchoring *World News Now* from 3 AM to 5 AM. During the day, he was reporting for ABC's *20/20* magazine news show. He was exhausted. So when ABC's entertainment division called him to offer him a job hosting *The Mole*, he agreed. In the reality series, fourteen competitors attempted to solve a series of tough physical and mental challenges to win $1 million, while a "mole" hidden among them tried to sabotage their efforts.

Cooper was criticized for leaving news reporting in 2000 to host the ABC reality series *The Mole*.

Cooper's role was to lead the competitors through the games, while sharing his personal observations about the competition and the players with the TV audience. When Cooper left the news division, many people in the business predicted he'd never work in news again, but he wasn't concerned. "Frankly, I didn't see much of a difference between the stuff that I was seeing on news shows and reality TV," he told *New York* magazine in September 2005.

Cooper stayed on *The Mole* for two seasons. Then, on September 11, 2001, two commercial airliners, hijacked by terrorists, crashed into the twin towers of the World Trade Center in New York City. A third airliner plowed into the Pentagon just outside Washington, D.C. A fourth was on its way to Washington, but the passengers were able to abort the terrorists' mission and crash the plane in a field in Shankesville, Pennsylvania. The world was forever changed. Cooper knew he had to get back to reporting news. In mid-September, a former *Channel One* colleague who had taken a job at CNN called and asked Cooper if he would be interested in going to Afghanistan for CNN to cover the impending American-led attack there. It was the beginning of America's "war on terror," which President George W. Bush had declared against Osama bin Laden and Afghanistan's Al Qaeda–friendly Taliban regime after the terrorist attacks on American soil. Cooper agreed to take the job. He joined CNN in December 2001.

FOUR

Cooper's Big Break

When Anderson Cooper arrived at CNN, the network made him its weekend anchor. He also contributed to the weekday early-morning news show *American Morning* with Paula Zahn. Although he hadn't originally intended to become an anchor, Cooper discovered that he enjoyed the challenge of coming up with questions for his guests on live television. He was very aware, though, that he didn't have the typical anchor's formal bearing or studied delivery. "I'm not the best TelePrompTer reader, and I say 'um' too much, and I stumble and I stutter a lot," he told *New York* magazine in 2005. But audiences seemed to love him.

Sexiest Man Alive

When Cooper started at CNN, he became known as much for his distinctive look as for his signature personal reporting style. In 2002 (and again in 2005), *People* magazine put Cooper on its Sexiest Men Alive list. A legion of Anderson Cooper fans emerged, dubbing themselves "Anderfans" and "Anderholics," and naming the object of their affection "Super Cooper." Anderson Cooper fan sites sprang up all over the Internet.

Cooper was flattered but surprised by all the attention. Far from the lanky, silver-haired sex symbol that his fans see, Cooper describes himself as "pale, skinny, and gray," according to a 2002 article in *People* magazine. He tries to keep his popularity in perspective, a skill he learned from his famous mother. "If you're not careful, you can become used to being treated as though you're special and begin to expect it. For a reporter, that's the kiss of death," he told *Interview* in 2004.

Anderson Cooper 360°

Cooper's performance on *American Morning* gained him enough public acclaim to convince CNN to give him his own show, *Anderson Cooper 360°*, in September 2003. The title refers to the depth of reporting: The show offers a 360° perspective of each story, showing the news from every angle. At a time

Anderson Cooper has become one of the most visible and recognizable anchors in cable news. In November 2004, he covered CNN's 2004 election night results in the New York City studio.

when most network news programs were attracting an older
audience (the median age of
network news viewers in 2002
hovered around sixty, according
to a 2006 report by the organization Project for Excellence in
Journalism), Cooper's show was
aimed at viewers eighteen to
fifty-four years old (the demographic prized by advertisers for
its spending power). To attract
that audience, *Anderson Cooper
360°* is fast-paced, in-depth, and
edgy. The first episode aired on
September 8, 2003, at 7 PM
Eastern standard time. It covered
a variety of news items and features, including President Bush's
speech asking for more money
from Congress to fund the Iraq
War, an update on the trial of
Michael Skakel (the Kennedy
cousin who in 2002 was con-
victed of murdering a childhood
friend in 1975), and the Dalai

Lama's visit to America. Future shows would include a similar mix of hard news and pop-culture features.

Although he was spending a considerable amount of time in the studio, Cooper still went out on the road to cover major news events. In June 2004, he traveled to Baghdad to report on the turnover of power from the U.S.-governed Coalition Provisional Authority to an interim Iraqi government. While there, he went on patrol with the U.S. Army's First Cavalry division and spent a day touring the country in a Black Hawk helicopter with U.S. ambassador L. Paul Bremer III, head of the Coalition Provisional Authority. As Cooper rode with Bremer, the helicopter jerked up and down, flying low to the ground to avoid possible rocket-propelled grenade fire, then jumping up to skirt power lines. On the morning that Cooper left Baghdad, an insurgent rocket slammed into the hotel next door to where he was staying. Another landed near the airport when he was boarding his plane to leave. When Cooper reported in dangerous territories, there were always close calls.

The danger was just as intense when Cooper returned to Iraq at the end of January 2005. He was there to cover the interim presidential elections, the country's first national general elections since U.S. forces had ousted Saddam Hussein from power in the spring of 2003. To get from the Baghdad airport to the Green Zone (the tightly guarded area in central Baghdad where U.S. troops and Iraqi leadership live and work), Cooper had to travel the 8-mile (12 km) strip of road the military calls Route Irish. Locals refer to it as "the most dangerous road in the world" because it is a constant target of insurgent suicide attacks and improvised explosive devices (IEDs). Cooper wanted to cover a story about Route Irish, but the armed guards accompanying him convinced him otherwise. The area is so perilous that they wanted to protect their own anonymity.

When he returned from Iraq, Cooper brought back a souvenir—a lacquered box on which a portrait of Saddam Hussein was painted. He often kept mementos of his travels, like a toy airplane that a Rwandan boy had fashioned out of Marlboro cigarette cartons and cookie boxes, and part of a wooden column from a palace in India. He kept these, along with his prized 1946 edition of the book *Don Quixote* and the *Hardy Boys* mysteries he'd treasured from childhood, in his 1,800 square-foot (167 square-meter) Manhattan loft apartment. Other reminders of his travels, including a piece of a car

Cooper's office is located in one of the eighty-story twin glass towers of the Time Warner Center in New York City.

that was blown up in Sarajevo during the Bosnian War, he kept at his office on the seventh floor of One Time Warner Center (Time Warner is the parent company of CNN) at Columbus Circle, overlooking New York's Central Park.

Tsunami

On December 26, 2004, one of the most powerful earthquakes in history, measuring 9.0 on the Richter scale, struck off the west coast of northern Sumatra in Indonesia. The massive earthquake ripped open a fault line in the Indian Ocean more than 700 miles (1,120 km) long, and created a series of giant undersea waves called tsunamis that spread out in all directions. Within just a few hours, the huge waves had killed more than 200,000 people—more people than in any other tsunami in recorded history—along the coasts of South Asia and East Africa.

A week later, Cooper traveled to Sri Lanka to cover the story. As he drove from the airport toward the affected areas, he saw piles of rubble and people digging through them with their bare hands, desperately searching for what they had lost. He and his crew slept in a hotel a few hours from the coast. They worked all day shooting stories and returned to the hotel to edit them until late each night. The devastation was so overwhelming that Cooper decided to

When Cooper arrived in Sri Lanka in early 2005, he saw the devastation that the tsunami had left behind.

focus on individual stories, rather than try to take in the entire scene. In one of his stories, Cooper went on a search for two children—Sunera, age seven; and Jinandari, age five—who had been missing since their parents' car was swept away by the giant wave. He carried their school photos with him to the local hospital, where the walls were covered with photos of the dead. The story Cooper was covering was one among thousands of stories of loss.

Recognition

Cooper's work in the TV news field has earned him praise from fans and colleagues, as well as several media awards. Here are some of the awards he has received:

- Bronze Telly, for his coverage of famine in Somalia—1993
- Emmy Award, for his coverage of Princess Diana's funeral—1997
- GLAAD Media Award for Outstanding TV Journalism, for his *20/20 Downtown* report on high school athlete Corey Johnson—2001
- National Headliners Award, for his coverage of the Southeast Asian tsunami—2005
- Peabody Award, for his coverage of Hurricane Katrina—2005
- Emmy Award, for his report on the famine in Niger—2006

Starving in Niger

When Cooper returned from Sri Lanka, he saw first-hand how his on-camera popularity was growing. Reporters were now calling *him* for interviews. Meanwhile at CNN, he was tapped to cover all the top stories. In March 2005, he went to Florida to cover the legal and political dispute over the right to end life support for Terri Schiavo, a woman who had been in a persistent vegetative state (a condition in which brain damage prevents a person from communicating or moving voluntarily) since 1990. In April 2005, he covered the funeral of Pope John Paul II live from Vatican City in Rome.

In late July, Cooper finally took a break and vacationed in Rwanda with some friends. He visited the African country's mountain gorillas and toured its genocide museum, later reflecting on the museum visit in *Dispatches from the Edge* as "not everyone's idea of fun, perhaps, but I've never been very good at taking time off." While in Rwanda, he saw a television news story about Niger, a desperately poor country in the northwestern part of the African continent. In 2004, a drought had hit Niger, and it was followed by a plague of locusts—events that had destroyed the previous year's crops and had put

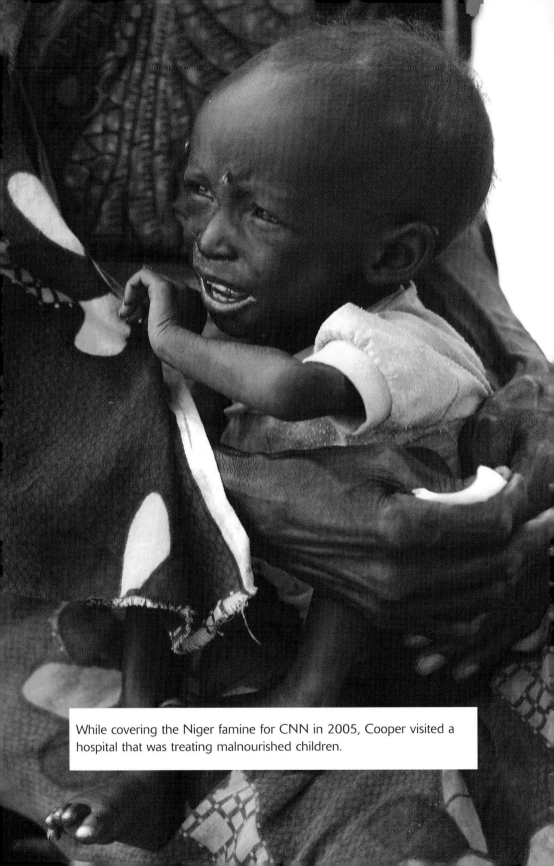

While covering the Niger famine for CNN in 2005, Cooper visited a hospital that was treating malnourished children.

some 3.5 million people at risk for starvation. Cooper asked CNN if he could travel there to cover the story for the network.

Cooper wanted to show people in the United States the reality of famine, especially for its youngest victims. He visited a hospital in Maradi, Niger, where mothers brought their malnourished children for help. Cooper's cameras rolled as infants died, one after another. He had seen death and devastation many times before as a reporter covering wars and natural disasters. Although he tried to stay emotionally uninvolved, the pain he was capturing in his stories was getting to him. "I used to think that some good would come of my stories, that someone might be moved to act because of what I'd reported," he wrote in *Dispatches from the Edge*. "I'm not sure I believe that anymore."

FIVE
A Voice in the Storm

Moving from war coverage to hurricane coverage didn't prove to be a big leap for Anderson Cooper. In both situations, "You're running toward what everyone else is running from," he wrote in the November 2004 issue of *Details*. The 2004 and 2005 hurricane seasons were extremely active. CNN sent Cooper out to cover six major hurricanes in that time span, including Hurricanes Charley and Frances, each of which dealt a serious blow to Florida in the late summer of 2004. While standing in the storms, trying to think of something to say other than "That wind is really blowing," or another cliché,

Cooper learned how much devastation wind and rain could leave behind. "It's easy to get caught up in all the excitement, easy to forget that while you are talking on TV, someone is cowering somewhere with their kids, or drowning or getting the roof ripped off their home," he wrote in the same *Details* issue.

Covering Katrina

The year 2005 holds the record for being the most active one for hurricanes. By the third week of August 2005, the National Hurricane Center had already named ten storms, and an eleventh storm was gaining force in the warm waters off the coast of the Bahamas. On August 24, it became a tropical storm, which meteorologists named Katrina. While Katrina churned in the Atlantic, Cooper was enjoying much calmer waters. He was spending time with friends, relaxing on a boat in the Adriatic Sea, off the coast of Croatia. Then an urgent message came through on his BlackBerry. It was his executive producer, David Doss, letting him know that he was needed back home.

Katrina strengthened into hurricane force on Thursday, August 25. It slammed into southern Florida, killing twelve people before moving out to the ocean again, this time over the warm waters of

the Gulf of Mexico, where it gained more strength. On Saturday, August 27, Cooper boarded a plane in Dubrovnik, Croatia, and headed for Houston, Texas. He landed in Houston on Sunday, August 28, and rented an SUV. While residents of the Gulf Coast tried to evacuate the area that authorities had identified as being in the hurricane's path, Cooper was trying to make his way into it. He planned to cover the violent storm from New Orleans, but Katrina's outer bands were already starting to move into the Gulf Coast, and the roads leading to New Orleans were blocked by debris. Consequently, Cooper hunkered down in Baton Rouge, Louisiana, to ride out the storm.

Early on the morning of Monday, August 29, Hurricane Katrina made landfall near Buras, Louisiana, which is about 60 miles (100 km) south-east of New Orleans. Although Baton Rouge is about 140 miles (225 km) to the north and farther inland from Buras, conditions there also began to deteriorate as the storm surged onshore. Power lines blew down, electricity outages were widespread, and

Cooper reports from the doorway of a New Orleans home that was badly damaged by Hurricane Katrina in August 2005.

In Gulfport, Mississippi, Hurricane Katrina moved this enormous casino barge from the water onto land.

roofs were ripped from buildings, but Cooper continued his report, standing soaked in his CNN slicker. By midday on Monday, the most destructive part of Katrina had passed through Louisiana and moved into Mississippi. Although Cooper and his crew were exhausted, they had to keep traveling to follow the story.

On Tuesday, August 30, they reached one of the hardest-hit areas: Gulfport, Mississippi. Although New Orleans was the focus of most of the news coverage after Hurricane Katrina made landfall, the beachfront city of Gulfport, like much of the Mississippi coastline, was utterly devastated. The only place Cooper could compare the extensive damage to was the large-scale devastation he had witnessed in Sri Lanka after the tsunami, he told *Maclean's* in

June 2006. He broadcast his report standing in front of a casino boat as long as a city block that the hurricane had washed up on land. Through huge gashes in the side of the boat, Cooper could see the slot machines that were still inside.

The following day, Cooper drove from Gulfport about 30 miles (48 km) west along the coast of Mississippi to Waveland. Miles of homes along the shoreline had been obliterated. Cooper grabbed his handheld recorder and followed the search-and-rescue efforts that were deployed in Waveland. He videotaped as small groups of rescuers went from door to door looking for victims of the storm. He saw bodies floating in the street with no one to retrieve them. He started asking on the air why the government wasn't doing more about the situation in the Gulf Coast region.

Besides the misery and despair Cooper witnessed while covering the storm's aftermath, he spotted surprising glimpses of his family history. This was, after all, the part of the country that his father had called home for much of his life. While in Meridian, Mississippi, Cooper's CNN crew got stuck on a road behind some downed trees. A group of local residents with chainsaws came to help them get through. These people turned out to be Anderson's cousins on his father's side. A few days later, when Cooper and his crew were in New Orleans, they parked their trailers on Canal Street, close to the old Maison Blanche department store where Cooper's father had worked as a teenager when the Cooper family had lived briefly in New Orleans during the 1940s.

The Interview That Changed Everything

On September 1, Cooper interviewed Louisiana senator Mary Landrieu, who was joining him by remote from Baton Rouge. He had no idea that he was going to be interviewing Senator Landrieu until a few minutes before they began, and so he had little time to prepare. He came up with most of his questions live during the interview. Cooper's anger and frustration, built up over three days of following the aftermath of Katrina and witnessing the lack of government response to the destruction and death, rushed to the surface. Although reporters try to distance themselves from their stories and remain objective, Cooper was having difficulty reining in his rage. When Landrieu complimented government efforts after the storm, he challenged her, saying, "I mean, there are people who want answers, and there are people who want someone to stand up and say, 'You know what? We should

have done more' . . . I mean, there are a lot of people here who are kind of ashamed of what is happening in this country right now . . . ashamed of what is happening in your state, certainly."

After they finished, Cooper feared that he had crossed the line and had offered too much of his own opinion, he later recalled in *Dispatches from the Edge*. But his emotions were already tightly woven into the story. When CNN came back to Cooper from a commercial break, the cameraman was focused on a shot of a pickup truck driving by. In the back of the truck a man was waving with pride a battered American flag that he had pulled from the storm wreckage. When the camera panned over to Cooper, he was crying.

Later, a *New York* magazine reporter asked Cooper whether he thought he went too far with Senator Landrieu. Cooper replied, "Yeah, I would prefer not to be emotional, and I would prefer not to get upset, but it's hard not to when you're surrounded by brave people who are suffering and in need." The public didn't think he went too far.

Cooper's September 1, 2005, interview with Senator Mary Landrieu of Louisiana after Hurricane Katrina marked a turning point in his career.

They loved his emotion and humanity, and they flooded the Internet with positive comments about the interview. "Was it possible for us to love Anderson Cooper more than we already did?" bloggers wrote on the Web site Gawker.com.

From Anchor to Superstar

The fans loved Cooper, and his television show's ratings were proof. During the first week of the Hurricane Katrina coverage, *Anderson Cooper 360°* had a 400 percent spike in viewership. CNN responded to the ratings increase by expanding Cooper's time slot from one hour to two hours in September 2005. In addition to hosting his regular show every weeknight, Cooper teamed up with venerable CNN anchor Aaron Brown as cohost of *NewsNight*, which aired from 10 PM to midnight.

Brown had been with CNN since 2001. On his very first day, he had anchored the network's 9/11 coverage. But just two months after partnering with Anderson Cooper, Brown was out. He left CNN, and network executives moved *Anderson Cooper 360°* into *NewsNight's* slot. The move shook up the entire network's schedule. Several other shows had to be moved to accommodate *Anderson Cooper 360°*. Cooper was no longer just an anchor; he was a star. His coverage of the famine in Niger, the aftermath of Hurricane Katrina, and other leading stories had put him at center stage in the news world. His ability to ask the questions that viewers really wanted answered struck a sympathetic chord with his audience. "There were literally hundreds of TV journalists at these events. Why is he the most talked about of them?" Jonathan Klein, president of CNN/United States, asked the *Washington Post* in November 2005. "That happens because a reporter has got that magical something." Klein regularly referred to Cooper as the "anti-anchor" and said the network couldn't ignore the audience's fervent response to him.

To promote Cooper as its new star, CNN launched an all-out media blitz, plastering his portrait on billboards, television commercials, print ads, and advertising banners on Internet blog sites. The ads showcased Cooper's strength: his ability to connect with his subjects. One ad showed Cooper on a beach in Southeast Asia after the tsunami, surrounded by children. The caption read: "I'll never forget the people I've met, the stories I've told, the places I've been. I am changed by the stories I do." The campaign was a huge turning point for CNN, which, until then, had never marketed any of its anchors as

Get the story firsthand.

ANDERSON COOPER 360

WEEKNIGHTS 10 PM ET

CNN

THE MOST TRUSTED NAME IN NEWS

"I'll never forget the people I've met, **the stories I've told, the places I've been.** I am changed by the stories I do."
—Anderson Cooper

ANDERSON COOPER 360

WEEKNIGHTS 10 PM CNN

THE MOST TRUSTED NAME IN NEWS

Following the ratings success of Cooper's Hurricane Katrina coverage, CNN launched a media campaign to promote its new star.

stars. In fact, media mogul Ted Turner, CNN's founder, used as one of his mottos for the network, "The news is the star."

CNN was hoping that Cooper could bring a much-desired younger audience to the 10 PM time slot. It appeared to work. By May 2006, ratings in the twenty-five-to-fifty-four-year-old demographic were up 53 percent from the previous year. The CBS news magazine show *60 Minutes* was also looking to attract a younger viewing audience when it asked Cooper to sign on as a part-time contributor in May 2006. He was one of the youngest reporters to be part of the program.

SIX

CHANGING THE FACE OF TELEVISION NEWS

By the age of thirty-eight, Anderson Cooper had met some of the most famous people in the entertainment and literary worlds. He had covered some of the biggest stories in recent years and had traveled all over the world. He hosted a popular news magazine show and had a huge fan following. Cooper knew he had a good story, and that story was his own. He collected his memories of family, personal loss, and his travels in his book, *Dispatches from the Edge: A Memoir of War, Disasters, and Survival*. HarperCollins published it in late May 2006. Cooper wrote the book, in part, because he didn't want people to forget about Hurricane Katrina after the floodwaters receded and the debris was cleared away. His popularity earned him a hefty advance for the book (reportedly $1 million) that Cooper mostly donated to charity, according to an article in the June 25, 2006, issue of the *Calgary Herald*.

Dispatches from the Edge moves back and forth through Cooper's personal and professional histories. He intermingles images of the widespread carnage in Sri Lanka after the 2005 tsunami with his memories of his father's death, and the story of a trip he took with his father to New Orleans when he was a child with descriptions of the disorder in that city after Hurricane Katrina. The book reveals Cooper as part of a new generation of reporters who don't just cover the story—they become part of the story. However, critics were mixed in their assessment of both the book and the reporting style it represents. In *Publishers Weekly*, a reviewer wrote, "Cooper is an intelligent, passionate man and he may be a terrific journalist." But, the reviewer continued, "he seems to place himself in front of his subjects." Nevertheless, CNN president Jonathan Klein continued to view Cooper's personal involvement as a big plus. "It's very important to help the audience make an emotional connection to a story,

DERSON COOPER   AND

DISPATCHES FROM THE EDGE

A MEMOIR OF WAR, DISASTERS, AND SURVIVAL

and some people just know how to do it instinctively," he told the *Boston Globe* in November 2005. "Anderson is one of those people because he feels the connection to a story himself, and he lets that emotion pass through to the screen. He's not afraid to show how much he cares."

A New Style of Reporting

News reporting has changed considerably over the years, and the line between hard news and entertainment has frequently blurred. In the 1960s and 1970s, Walter Cronkite anchored the evening news on CBS with a somber tone and a straight-forward delivery. Today, anchors chat casually with each other and with their guests, and they are less hesitant to introduce their personal opinions into the discussion. *Anderson Cooper 360°* is a model for this new style of journalism. Cooper is not only the anchor, but he is also the central focus. The show itself blends hard news with features in a much faster-paced format than most traditional news shows.

Cooper shares stories about personal loss and his professional life on the road in his 2006 memoir.

Part of the program's appeal for younger viewers has been its celebrity exclusives. One of Cooper's biggest coups occurred on June 20, 2006, when he interviewed Angelina Jolie. The actress and humanitarian, who is usually reticent about giving television interviews, contacted Cooper because of his interest in Africa. It was her first interview after having given birth to Shiloh Nouvel Jolie-Pitt, her

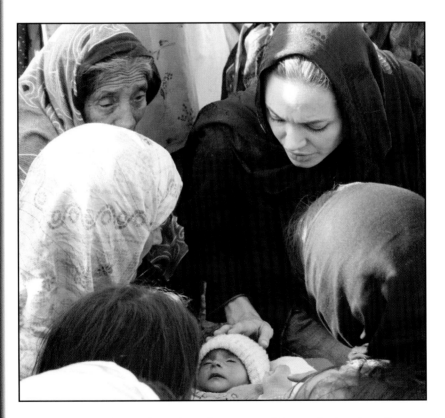

In June 2006, Cooper interviewed actress and humanitarian Angelina Jolie, who is seen here in Pakistan in 2005. Jolie's interview with Cooper was one of the few television interviews she has given.

daughter with actor Brad Pitt, in the previous month. Jolie took up much of the show's two-hour airtime, discussing her role as goodwill ambassador for the United Nations Refugee Agency and introducing viewers to the plight of the refugees. The following day, singer-actress Cher joined Cooper. She discussed her efforts to get better helmets for U.S. Marines serving in Iraq and Afghanistan. Celebrity interviews such as these garnered a great deal of media attention, with everyone from bloggers to media watchers reporting on them. However, Cooper's credibility came under fire from doing these entertainment-related stories, just as it had when he hosted *The Mole.*

Celebrity interviews were only a small part of Cooper's repertoire, though. He never stopped reporting the top news stories and major world events. In September 2006, CNN featured Cooper in its five-year anniversary tribute to September 11. Rather than putting him in New York for the story, they sent him to Afghanistan, an area that remained unstable even after the United States and the North Atlantic Treaty Organization (NATO) ousted the Taliban regime from power in late 2001. Cooper and his crew had set up along the Afghan-Pakistani border to watch U.S. troops hold their own commemorative event for 9/11, when the troops came under rocket fire. The CNN cameras continued to roll as soldiers behind Cooper scrambled for cover. Ever calm under fire, Cooper simply explained to viewers that he needed to stop the report and headed to a bunker for shelter.

An Uncharted Path

In the television news business, the traditional path for an anchor is to work his or her way up from local reporter to network reporter to network news anchor. Dan Rather, the former *CBS Evening News* anchor, began his career in 1950 as a reporter for the Associated Press and United Press International (both large news agencies that contribute reports to newspapers across the country and worldwide). He first gained national attention when he covered the assassination of President John F. Kennedy in 1963. Rather then served as a CBS White House correspondent before finally making it into the anchor's chair in 1981. Former *NBC News* anchor Tom Brokaw started out in 1962 working in local news in Omaha, Nebraska. NBC hired him as a correspondent in 1966, but Brokaw didn't get promoted into the anchor's seat until the mid-1980s. Dan Rather, Tom Brokaw, and

Dan Rather (*second from left*), pictured here in 1973, and other network news anchors of his generation worked as reporters for many years before being promoted to anchors.

others of their generation had years of reporting experience behind them before they were promoted to prime-time news anchors. That experience helped them convey a sense of trust in the anchor's chair, which kept viewers loyal to the TV network's news broadcast.

Viewers today seem to trust Cooper, although he took an uncharacteristic path to becoming a television anchor. When he couldn't get a job in

TV news, he created his own assignments, setting out abroad with a borrowed camera to report on stories in Burma, Rwanda, and many other perilous locations. After reporting for a while, he took a career detour and became host of the reality-TV series *The Mole*. Then he became host of the fast-paced news and features program *Anderson Cooper 360°*. Despite his unusual career path, Cooper became one of the most visible and well-liked anchors on cable news.

Although he ardently followed network news as a child, Cooper adopted a very individual reporting style. He says he never looks at the news he's covering as stories, or the people he interviews as characters. Instead, he sees them as real people with real, and often harrowing, experiences to share. It is this involved, deeply personal reporting style that has helped make him the popular news figure that he is today.

Although Cooper has always had a passion for reporting, he's never had a firm plan in place for his career. If someone had asked him the typical question, "Where do you see yourself in ten years?" during a job interview, he probably wouldn't have had an answer. But he loves what he does for a living, and his viewers love him. They've turned him into a pop-culture icon, with Web sites and blogs devoted to his hair, his love life, and his work. In 2006, he was featured on the cover of *Vanity Fair*, and he made guest appearances on *Oprah*, *Late Night with David Letterman*, and *The Tonight Show*. Despite his many fans and all the media attention he's received, Cooper says he doesn't believe all the hype about himself. He also doesn't give in to celebrity excesses, still preferring to ride the subway to work every day (although he does now travel with a bodyguard, following a few run-ins with overzealous fans).

The Changing Face of Television News

The television news business has changed dramatically in the twenty-first century. In the past, most people who watched TV got their news from one of three networks: NBC, CBS, or ABC. Today viewers have an ever-increasing number of news options available to them. On cable television alone, viewers can choose from straightforward news programs such as *The Situation Room* with Wolf Blitzer (CNN); opinion-based shows, like *The O'Reilly Factor* with Bill O'Reilly (Fox News Channel); and irreverent news parodies such as *The Daily Show with Jon Stewart* (Comedy Central). It's even possible to

Television viewers now have a wide array of news coverage to choose from, including the satirical program *The Daily Show with Jon Stewart*. Stewart *(right)* interviewed Democratic presidential candidate John Kerry in August 2004.

watch the news without turning on a television set. People can now call up news segments on the Internet, read news blogs, or even download the news to their iPods.

Because they have so many choices, many television news viewers are looking for something different from the traditional network newscast. They have embraced Cooper's more personal style of reporting. His method has not only made him hugely popular with his viewers, but it also has given him a kind of influence few reporters experience. In *Dispatches from the Edge*, Cooper recalled what a man in New Orleans had said to him in the aftermath of Hurricane Katrina: "You have the power of a thousand bulldozers." Although he believes that assessment is a bit of an overstatement, Cooper

Cooper received an Emmy Award in September 2006 for his CNN report on the famine in Niger.

finally does have a sense that people are watching him, and that the words and images he reports really do have the power to change things for the better.

May 17, 1794 Cornelius "Commodore" Vanderbilt is born in Port Richmond, New York.

February 20, 1924 Gloria Vanderbilt is born in Newport, Rhode Island.

September 1, 1927 Wyatt Cooper is born in Quitman, Mississippi.

January 27, 1965 Carter Vanderbilt Cooper is born in New York City.

June 3, 1967 Anderson Hays Cooper is born in New York City.

January 5, 1978 Wyatt Cooper dies of a heart attack at age fifty.

1984 Anderson graduates from the Dalton School.

July 22, 1988 Carter Vanderbilt Cooper commits suicide.

Spring 1989 Anderson graduates from Yale University.

December 1991 Anderson travels to Burma with a borrowed video camera to shoot his first report.

1995 The ABC television network hires Anderson Cooper as a correspondent.

1997 Cooper wins an Emmy for his coverage of Princess Diana's funeral.

2000 Cooper hosts the ABC reality-TV show *The Mole*.

December 2001 CNN hires Cooper to anchor the weekend news.

2002 *People* magazine declares Cooper one of the "Sexiest Men Alive."

September 8, 2003 *Anderson Cooper 360°*, an unconventional news program, premieres.

January 2005 Cooper covers the aftermath of the South Asia tsunami in Sri Lanka.

September 1, 2005 Cooper interviews Louisiana senator Mary Landrieu after Hurricane Katrina.

November 2005 *Anderson Cooper 360°* is expanded to a two-hour time slot.

May 2006 Cooper's memoir, *Dispatches from the Edge: A Memoir of War, Disasters, and Survival,* is published.

GLOSSARY

châteaux Castles, country homes, or mansions in France.

coup d'état The sudden, often violent overthrow of a country's government by a small group.

demographics The age and other statistics related to a human population that are used to identify a market.

demo reel A videotape, submitted to a potential employer, that showcases a reporter's abilities on camera.

dyslexia The impairment of a person's ability to read.

epitaph The words inscribed on someone's tombstone.

ethnic cleansing The killing of one ethnic group to increase the population of another ethnic group.

freelancer A person who is self-employed and gets paid by the project.

genocide The systematic, planned killing of an entire racial, political, cultural, or religious group.

gravitas A serious or dignified demeanor; weightiness.

insurgent A person who rebels against an established government or civil authority.

levee An embankment that is built to protect land from flooding.

magnate A wealthy and powerful business executive or tycoon.

malaria An infectious disease that is transmitted by mosquitoes.

melatonin A pigment that affects skin and hair color.

obelisk A tall four-sided stone shaft that has a pyramid-shaped top.

paparazzi Freelance photographers who aggressively chase celebrities so that they can take candid shots.

patriarch The male head of a family.

periauger A two-masted boat.

persistent vegetative state A condition, caused by damage to the brain, in which a person is awake but unable to communicate.

philanthropy The active effort to donate money to help people who are less fortunate.

ratings The estimates of the percentage of people who listen to a particular radio program or watch a certain television show.

socialite A person who is socially important.

tsunami A shoreward-bound series of large waves that can be produced by an underwater disturbance such as an earthquake, landslide, or volcanic eruption.

FOR MORE INFORMATION

ABC News
7 West 66th Street
New York, NY 10023
(212) 456-7777
Web site: http://abcnews.go.com

Anderson Cooper 360°
One Time Warner Center
New York, NY 10019
(212) 484-8000
http://www.cnn.com/CNN/Programs/
   anderson.cooper.360

Biltmore Estate
1 Approach Road
Asheville, NC 28803
(800) 624-1575
Web site: http://www.biltmore.com

Channel One Network
4455 Connecticut Avenue NW, Suite 225
Washington, DC 20008

(202) 587-4101

Web site: http://www.channelone.com

Museum of Television and Radio

25 West 52nd Street

New York, NY 10019

(212) 621-6800

Web site: http://www.mtr.org

National Association of Broadcasters

1771 N Street NW

Washington, DC 20036

(202) 429-5300

Web site: http://www.nab.org

Newseum

1101 Wilson Boulevard

Arlington, VA 22209

(888) NEWSEUM (639-7386)

Web site: http://www.newseum.org

Radio-Television News Directors Association &
   Foundation (RTNDA)

1600 K Street NW, Suite 700

Washington, DC 20006-2838

(202) 659-6510
Web site: http://www.rtnda.org

U.S. Department of Labor, Bureau of Labor Statistics
Division of Occupational Employment Statistics and
    Employment Projections
2 Massachusetts Avenue NE, Suite 2135
Washington, DC 20212-0001
(202) 691-5700
Web site: http://www.bls.gov/home.htm

Yale University
Office of Admissions
38 Hillhouse Avenue
New Haven, CT 06511
(203) 432-9392
Web site: http://www.yale.edu/index.html

Web Sites

Due to the changing nature of Internet links, Rosen
Publishing has developed an online list of Web sites
related to the subject of this book. This site is updated
regularly. Please use this link to access the list:

http://www.rosenlinks.com/cp/anco

For Further Reading

CNN News. *Hurricane Katrina: CNN Reports: State of Emergency*. Riverside, NJ: Andrews McMeel Publishing, 2005.

Cooper, Anderson. *Dispatches from the Edge: A Memoir of War, Disasters, and Survival*. New York, NY: HarperCollins Publishers, 2006.

Croffut, W. A. *Vanderbilts and the Story of Their Fortune*. Whitefish, MT: Kessinger Publishing, 2003.

Facts on File. *Journalism* (Ferguson's Careers in Focus). New York, NY: Facts on File, 2005.

Henderson, Harry. *Power of the News Media*. New York, NY: Facts on File, 2004.

Parks, Peggy J. *Careers for the Twenty-First Century— News Media*. San Diego, CA: Lucent Books, 2002.

Patterson, Jerry E. *The Vanderbilts*. New York, NY: Harry N. Abrams, 1989.

Stasz, Clarice. *The Vanderbilt Women*. Lincoln, NE: iUniverse, 2000.

Vanderbilt, Arthur T. *Fortune's Children*. New York, NY: Harper Paperbacks, 1991.

Vanderbilt, Gloria. *A Mother's Story*. New York, NY: Alfred A. Knopf, Inc., 1996.

BIBLIOGRAPHY

Barron, James. "Vanderbilt Son Recalled as a Man with High Ideals." *New York Times*, July 27, 1988, p. B-5.

Cooper, Anderson. "Books that Made a Difference to Anderson Cooper." *O, The Oprah Magazine*, Vol. 6, No. 7, July 2005, pp. 130–131.

Cooper, Anderson. *Dispatches from the Edge: A Memoir of Wars, Disaster, and Survival*. New York, NY: HarperCollins, 2006.

Cooper, Anderson. "My Brother's Suicide." *Details*, September 2003. Retrieved September 4, 2006 (http://www.cnn.com/2005/US/08/16/brother/index.html).

Cooper, Anderson. "The Perfect Storm." *Details*, November 2004. Retrieved September 4, 2006 (http://www.cnn.com/2005/US/09/27/perfect.storm/index.html).

George, Lianne. "Anderson Cooper Feels Your Pain." *Maclean's*, Vol. 119, June 2006, pp. 66–67.

Goldfarb, Brad. "Anderson Cooper." *Interview*, Vol. 34, No. 9, October 2004, pp. 122–126.

"Special Edition: Hurricane Katrina." *Anderson Cooper 360°*. CNN.com. September 1, 2005.

Retrieved December 6, 2006 (http://transcripts.cnn.com/TRANSCRIPTS/0509/01/acd.01.html).

Stasz, Clarice. *The Vanderbilt Women*. New York, NY: St. Martin's Press, 1991.

Vanderbilt, Arthur T. *Fortune's Children: The Fall of the House of Vanderbilt*. New York, NY: William Morrow and Company, Inc., 1989.

Vanderbilt, Gloria. *A Mother's Story*. New York, NY: Alfred A. Knopf, Inc., 1996.

Van Meter, Jonathan. "Unanchored." *New York Magazine*, September 19, 2005. Retrieved September 4, 2006 (http://www.newyorkmetro.com/nymetro/news/features/14301/).

INDEX

C
A
R
E
E
R

P
R
O
F
I
L
E
S

About the Author

Stephanie Watson is a writer and editor based in Atlanta, Georgia. She is the author of several young-adult books on topics ranging from history to health and science. She earned her bachelor of science degree in mass communications from Boston University. Before embarking on her writing career, Watson worked as a television writer and producer.

Photo Credits

Cover, pp. 35, 60–61, 94–95 © Paul Hawthorne/Getty Images; p. 5 © Pete Mitchell/Wireimage.com; pp. 11, 15, 17 © Hulton Archive/ Getty Images; p. 13 © Edwin Levick/Hulton Archives/Getty Images; p. 22 © Tim Boxer/Getty Images; p. 26 © Jack Robinson/ Hulton Archive/Getty Images; p. 28 © Susan Wood/Getty Images; p. 30 © Joe Raedle/Getty Images; pp. 33, 72 © AP/Wide World Photos; p. 39 © Ron Galella/Wireimage.com; p. 40 shutterstock. com; p. 46 © Roselle Assirelli/AFP/Getty Images; p. 47 © Eric Feferberg/AFP/Getty Images; pp. 48–49 © Janek Skarzynski/AFP/ Getty Images; p. 52 www.news.navy.mil; p. 53 © ABC/Everett Collection; p. 55 © Everett Collection; p. 64 © Stephen Chernin/ Getty Images; p. 65 © Paula Bronstein/Getty Images; p. 68 © Daniel Berehulak/Getty Images; pp. 74–75 © Marianne Todd/ Getty Images; p. 78 © Mike Theiler/Getty Images; p. 88 © J. Redden/UNHCR/Getty Images; p. 91 © Getty Images; p. 96 © Marc Bryan-Brown/Wireimage.com.

Designer: Tahara Anderson; **Editor:** Kathy Campbell; **Photo Researcher:** Amy Feinberg